Address of the Board of Trustees of the Protestant Episcopal Theological Seminary of Maryland to the members of the church in this diocess [sic].

John Johns

ADDRESS

OF THE

BOARD OF TRUSTEES

OF THE

PROTLSTANT EPISCOPAL

Theological Seminary

OF

MARYLAND,

TO

THE MEMBERS OF THE CHURCH

IN

THIS DIOCESS.

———

GEORGETOWN, D C.
JAMES C DUNN, PRINTER.
...
1822.

ADDRESS.

———

BRETHREN.

THE Great Head of the Church has in his infinite wisdom, so constituted his kingdom upon earth, that the exertions of his people, in reliance on his blessing and assistance, are necessary to promote its extension and prosperity. Those supernatural communications which the sacred volume represents as essential to qualify men for the services of the altar, are not designed to supersede such human efforts, as may prepare the minister for an intelligent and respectable performance of the high and responsible duties which are connected with his office. This statement is sustained by the formulary of our church, which not only requires that the candidate for orders should profess "a trust that he is inwardly moved by the Holy Ghost," but "also, that upon examination, he be found apt and meet for his learn- "ing, to exercise his ministry to the honour of God,—the edifying of his church." The members of our communion have long been con- vinced of the importance of this consideration, and at an early period, after the church was duly organized here, the education of young men for her ministry claimed her attention. A variety of circumstances, for a long time rendered it impracticable to accomplish this desirable object.—It has been of necessity delayed from year to year, but it has never been abandoned. The period, we humbly hope, has now arrived, when the prayers of the pious will be answered, and this design, which has so long been projected, will be fully realized.— Those evils which depressed and wasted our zion have, in an encou- raging degree, been removed. Those who left her sanctuaries thro' necessity, are returning of choice.—The number and the strength of her children, have, within a few years, been greatly increased.— These are animating considerations, and whilst they increase the call for duly qualified ministers, they also furnish the promise of means for facilitating the improvement of our candidates in those branches of human 'earning which may, under God, enlarge the sphere of their usefulness among their fellow-men. To put these resources of the church in requisition, and realize the advantages which they would afford, has for some time past been regarded as quite feasible, and we find that this subject was formally brought before the General Convention which met at New York, A D 1817 It was then resolved to establish a Theological Seminary in the city of New York, and a committee was appointed to carry this resolution into operation. Comparatively little, however, was done in this business before the meeting of the General Convention of 1820, which assembled in Philadelphia, when it was deemed expedient to remove the Seminary from New York, to New Haven. With regard to this removal, there was a strongly marked division of opinion and feeling among the members of the Convention. The remoteness of New Haven from many sections of our church, the expenses connected with the attainment of an education there, by those who would be under the necessity of traversing our states to reach the Seminary, were urged as serious objections The propriety of the Convention's legislating on the subject of a General Seminary was questioned, or granting this, the expediency of such an institution for the whole church was disputed, and it was well known to be the opinion of the venerable presiding Bishop, that Diocesan Schools would be preferable These difficulties, however, were all obviated by a communication from the House of Bishops, which silenced opposition to the General Seminary, by an explicit declaration that each Diocess would still be left at liberty to make such arrangement for the education of candidates within its own bounds, as the Convention of such Diocess might think proper.—This communication was in the following words· "The House of Bishops inform the House of Clerical "and Lay Deputies that, in concurring in the resolutions relative to "the Theological Seminary, and its removal from the city of New "York, they deem it proper to declare, that they do not mean by "this concurrence to interfere with any plan now contemplated, or "that hereafter may be contemplated, in any Diocess or Diocesses, "for the establishment of theological institutions or professorships" —Such a declaration was truly gratifying to those persons who, though not hostile to a General Seminary, were aware that, let it be located where it might, it must be so remote from many of our Dioceses, as to preclude their indigent students from the privileges which it would afford, and who believed that Diocesan Institutions, would supply this defect and answer other desirable purposes which could not be attained by a General Seminary.

Soon after this Convention, which furnished the occasion for this expression of the views of the House of Bishops, we find two of our largest and most respectable Dioceses acting in accordance with this communication. The Diocess of Virginia, unanimously, it is believed, determined to establish a state Seminary at Williamsburg, and efficient measures were adopted to carry their resolution into immediate operation. In the Diocess of New York, a similar plan was originated, and the most energetic efforts were made to ensure its success. Maryland had as yet done nothing. The agents for the General Seminary at New Haven, had been on to solicit aid, but, if we may judge from the result of their application the institution which they represented had awakened, and was likely to awaken, but little interest in Maryland, for on reverting to their published subscription list, it does not appear that any thing had been contributed by this Diocess

Such was the situation of things, when the Convention of this state met in Baltimore, in June, A. D. 1821. It was then ascertained that there was a disposition on the part of the church in Virginia, to solicit our co-operation in the Seminary, which they had resolved to establish, and, on the strength of this discovery, the following preamble and resolution were laid before our Convention by one of its lay delegates :—" Whereas the Convention of the church in the " Diocess of Virginia, has determined to establish a Theological " School in the College of Williamsburg, with the consent of the " Society of that institution, and the faculty of this respectable Semi- " nary, have generously offered gratuitous instruction to all *bona fide* " students of theology who may repair to it, the Convention also " recommends to the Board of Trustees of the projected School, to " correspond with the standing committee of this Diocess, to ascer- " tain whether the members of our church are disposed to co-ope- " rate in this important measure: Influenced by an uniform disposi- " tion to promote any measure which may in any degree advance the

"spiritual influence of the church and the blessings of our holy
" religion, this Convention cannot withhold their approbation of the
" laudable efforts of the Convention of the Diocese of Virginia, for
" the attainment of these important objects Therefore, *Resolved*,
" That this Convention approve of the design of the Convention of
" the state of Virginia, to establish a Theological School at Williams-
" burg in that state, and recommend it to the patronage and support
" of the members of the church in this Diocess "—Such were the
preamble and resolution then offered After some discussion, it
was on motion, resolved, that the further consideration of it be defer-
red to the next Convention, and it was thus transmitted on our printed journals to the vestries of the different parishes, and laid before
them for consideration during the ensuing year

At the expiration of the year, when the convention of this state
met in June last, in St. John's church in the City of Washington, this
subject was called up as constituting part of the unfinished business
on the journals —The mover of the resolution, then came forward
with a *substitute* for the one which he had offered, the effect of the
substitute was simply this·—that instead of providing for the education of our candidates by a co-operation with Virginia, we should
endeavour to make a similar provision at home, in our own Diocess,
and subject to the government of our own Convention.—The substitute was in these words.—" Whereas the calls of the church in
" this section of the country, for ministers rightly qualified to divide
" the word of truth, are loud and frequent, and are daily becoming
" more urgent and imperious, and since it is desirable to furnish
" every facility to those who are solicitous of being duly prepared
" for the high and responsible office of the gospel ministry, and as
" the experience of the church in all ages, has born the most ample
" testimony to the admirable tendency of well regulated theological
" schools. to promote this object, therefore, *Resolved*, by the Conven-
" tion of the Protestant Episcopal Church in the Diocess of Mary-
" land, that it is now expedient, in reliance on the blessing of God
" for success, to establish a local Theological Seminary.

" And it is further *Resolved*, That a committee consisting of five
" members, three of whom shall be of the clergy, and the rest of the
" laity, be elected by ballot, to report to this Convention, a constitu-
" tion for the government of said Seminary "

The Convention by which this resolution was considered, was large and respectable, the subject was agitated with great ability, "the discussion was long and minute, and was carried on in a spirit and temper suited to the interesting occasion;"—at the conclusion of the debate, the substitute was adopted "by a majority which astonished and elevated its friends." In taking the question, it was requested that the clergy and laity should vote separately, and the yeas and nays were called for; when it appeared that there were twenty-three of the clergy in the affirmative, and but eight in the negative. Of the laity, there were nineteen in the affirmative and eleven in the negative, thus giving a majority of fifteen clergymen and eight laymen in favour of the resolution, and, on joint vote, a majority of twenty-three, for on dividing the Convention, it will be found that there were forty-two members in the affirmative and only nineteen in the negative,—of these nineteen, several have since declared that they voted as they did, not because they were opposed to the resolution, but because they wished it postponed for another year.

Under the authority of this most encouraging concurrence among the members of the Convention, a committee was immediately chosen by ballot to draft a constitution This committee had before them constitutions of similar seminaries which were already established, and by the aid of these they were enabled, according to the resolution under which they were appointed, to report the result of their labours before the Convention rose They had the satisfaction to find that the constitution which they handed in, was favourably received and viewed in the light in which it was drafted—*as a general outline*, formed upon *general* principles, sufficiently full for the inception of their undertaking, and yet open for such additions as time and experience might prove to be proper The only principle to which any exception was taken, was that which is contained in the eighth article, which provides that none of the proceedings of the Board of Trustees shall be annulled unless by the vote of two-thirds of the members present at the Convention This provision occasioned a short debate, but the Convention decided that it should stand as reported by the committee.

According to this constitution, as then adopted, the Convention proceeded to the election of a Board of Trustees. With a view of discharging the duties assigned them as speedily as possible, an effort was made to have the first meeting of the Board before its members separated to their different places of residence. Nine of the thirteen Trustees accordingly assembled in Washington on the Monday morning after the Convention adjourned It was ascertained, however, that two of the members had not received their invitation,—there was therefore *no* meeting of the Board, there was an *attempt to have a meeting*, but there was none, either *formal* or *informal*.

The constitution of the Seminary has since been printed, and means have been taken to distribute it through the Diocess. A copy has been forwarded to the Bishop, who is ex-officio President of the Board

Although it was ascertained that our Diocesan was not favourable to the Seminary which the Convention had determined to establish, yet the Board were not prepared for the letter which he has since addressed to them It is always unpleasant to differ, let the dissenting party be as small as it may In the present instance, the Board had hoped that the Bishop, with the few of the clergy and laity who thought as he did, would have yielded their private opinion to the voice of the Convention, and that the manner in which the institution should be conducted would soon conciliate their feelings, and number them among its warmest patrons This hope has, however, with regard to the right reverend gentleman alluded to, proved fallacious In his communication to the Board, he has declined acting with them, and refused to discharge the duties of the honourable station to which the Convention appointed him,—he has also accompanied this communication with remarks and strictures on the proceedings of the Convention, the constitution which it adopted, and the acts of its Board of Trustees. These the Board would most cheerfully pass in respectful silence; but finding that they are given to the public in an unusual and unexpected shape, that they are making their way through the Diocess under form of a *Pastoral Letter*, they feel bound in duty to the Convention under whose authority they act, to come forward and perform the unpleasant task of defending its measures against the charges of its President We wish it distinctly understood, that in discharging this duty, we are combatting *principles and objections*, principles and objections which we can show to be mistaken and groundless,—which are not only in the face of the deliberate decision of our Diocesan government, but also of our General Convention, and which are opposed to the opinion and the practice of other Diocesses and their Bishops. Some of those objections we now proceed to state. We take them from a printed form, entitled "A Pastoral Letter, addressed to the Members of the Protestant Episcopal Church in the Diocess of Maryland" This letter is, in substance, a caution against aiding or abetting "the wild and impracticable scheme" of establishing the contemplated Theological Seminary. The pamphlet commences thus .—"In all matters in which either the character or the interests of the church may be involved, I deem it my duty to give you all the information I possess, and particularly when measures are urged or schemes devised which I believe to be *incompatible with her principles, and may endanger her peace*" On the 13th page, 11th line, the following sentence occurs   " And the present plan of erecting a Theological Seminary, independent of the general one, I view as *counteracting that authority,* (the authority of the church) *and opening a door for errors and divisions of the most destructive kind*" On the 23d page, 8th line, these words are found — " This plan, then, is not only *unconstitutional,* but *hasty and ill-arranged.*"

In these quotations, which might be multiplied, the contemplated Seminary is pronounced to be unconstitutional in its nature, disorganizing in its tendency, and indigested and ill-formed in its character.

With regard to its *unconstitutionality* This charge we are prepared to meet and repel with authority which cannot be questioned and by facts which cannot be gainsaid   That each Diocess has the right to establish a Seminary of its own, has, as we have already seen, been most unequivocally declared to be the opinion of the House of Bishops—(see page 4.) On the construction of this expression of their sentiments, there can be but one opinion. We submit it to the good sense of every individual under whose notice it may fall, subjoining no comment but that which the following facts afford.   Let it therefore be recollected, that immediately after the publication of this opinion of the House of Bishops, Virginia formed her Diocesan School Did the church view this act as

B

unconstitutional? Did she pronounce it an act in opposition to the authority on which the General Seminary then rested? We hear not the slightest murmur of disapprobation We see no movement to arrest these efforts. We see a movement in the North, but not in hostility to Virginia New York came forward, avowed its approbation of the course pursued by the Southern Diocess, and immediately proceeded to establish a similar institution on a larger scale within its own bounds We will now show you the views and the feelings of the right reverend Bishop of New York on this important point We quote from his pastoral letter, published A D 1820 "The *right of every Diocess* to provide for the theological " education of candidates for orders, subject only to the provisions " of the general canons of the church, *cannot be questioned!* The " ecclesiastical authority of every Diocess is responsible for the " admission of persons as candidates for holy orders, who in their " state of preparation, are under the charge of that authority, and " amenable to it *It is impossible for a moment to doubt the right* " of any Diocess to make *any* arrangements which it may deem " proper, in consistency with the general canons of the church, for " the instruction and aid of candidates for orders who are under its " charge No act of the General Convention has ever contravened " this right. To prevent, however, all misapprehension on this sub- " ject, both the *right and the probability of its exercise,* were expli- " citly stated by the New York Deputation in the House of Clerical " and Lay Deputies, and in the House of Bishops, the following " declaration (see page 4) was adopted, as the condition on the part " of that House, of concurrence in the resolutions relative to the " Seminary at New Haven." Such are the words of Bishop Hobart Language cannot be more express—" The right cannot be questioned—it is impossible for a moment to doubt it." But that it is possible to question the position, that right reverend gentleman will now discover, to his utter astonishment; that it is possible, not only to doubt this right, but to declare that it does not exist

The Bishop of New York was not singular in his views of this subject The venerable presiding Bishop of the House of Bishops not only held, that Diocesan Seminaries were constitutional, but gave them a decided preference, and in the General Convention which resolved to establish a General Seminary, he rather yielded than changed his opinion, with that characteristic meekness which has endeared him to his clergy and to all who know him, he relinquished his individual sentiments to those of the majority of his brethren. Bishop Hobart, in his pastoral address alluded to, observes that "the following extracts from letters of Bishop White, "the venerable presiding Bishop, will unequivocally show the view "entertained in that House on this subject generally and particular- "ly with regard to an institution in New York" Extract. "That "full provision was made for the allowance of Diocesan Schools, "*I well remember*, and that the provision was *before* the passing "of what came from the other House, must be evident from this, "that otherwise it would not have been passed by us without debate, "and unanimously, if at all. As to New York, I know not how the "design of a Diocesan School could have been more explicitly de- "clared and acquiesced in, than was done in the House of Bishops" Such were the views of Bishop White. That they have not changed, we assert with confidence

One occurrence more, and we dismiss this point After the General Seminary had been removed from New York to New Haven, and the Diocesan Seminary in New York had been established, the legacy of the late Mr Sherrard became a matter of litigation between these two institutions, and the late special General Convention was called to endeavour to effect a compromise What ground was there taken? Was it contended that the Diocesan School of New York was unconstitutional—that it had no legal existence—and consequently could have no shadow of a claim to the legacy under consideration? No one ever dreamed of taking this stand. The School of New York was recognized as lawfully constituted, and the very constitution proposed by the Deputies of that Diocess, as the "sine qua non" of union, was, with a trifling exception, acceded to by the General Convention, and in compliance with it, the General Seminary was again removed and placed in New York, under the regulations which the influence of that state was pleased to prescribe If this be not a recognition of the constitutionality of the New York Diocesan School, actions have no meaning, and if it be constitutional for New York to establish a local Theological School, we have yet to learn why Maryland may not If the right be granted in one case, we cannot conceive why it should be denied in the other

We have thus, we think, shown that the House of Bishops have decided in our favour, that we have Virginia and New York as precedents, that Bishops White and Hobart have individually advocated our cause, and that the General Convention has, by its public acts, recognized the constitutionality of Diocesan Seminaries

With regard to the *expediency* of such institutions, and their influence upon the unity of the church, we are perfectly willing to appear with the sentiments and the language of the learned Bishop from whose pastoral letter we have already made a long quotation " It can hardly be supposed," says Bishop Hobart, " that the various " Diocesses that are or may be established, throughout this immense " continent, will unite in the support of one theological institution , " or that it will be practicable for candidates for orders to come to " one place for instruction, from all parts of the union. The expe- " rience of a very respectable religious communion, confirms this " reasoning from the general principles of human nature. The " Presbyterian church has a Theological Seminary at Princeton , " but a Synod of that church, in the western part of this state, have " established one, and another is contemplated by the Synod of Ten- " nessee.

" The propriety of the General Convention's legislating on the " establishment and regulation of a General Seminary, has been " doubted by many of the best friends of the church   The moment " that body governs too much, or extends its enactments to subjects " on which there are clashing views and interests, the peace and " union of the church are endangered   That the General Conven- " tion should confine its legislation to those matters that are abso- " lutely necessary to preserve the different parts of the church as " one body, is the principle which the venerable presiding Bishop " of our church states, as the principle which should be strictly ob- " served , and doubtless in conformity with this principle, and from " an apprehension of the collisions which might occur from attempts " by parties of different views, to obtain the control of the general " institution, he has always expressed his opinion in favour of pro- " vision being made by the different Diocesses, for the education of " candidates for orders. The very attempt to preserve unity of

" theological opinions, by a general institution under the authority of
" the Convention, would lead to collisions and to separations Here,
" too, the experience of other denominations may guide us The
" Presbyterian theological institutions, in the western part of this
" state and in Tennessee, I am credibly informed, are established
" by those who are not favourable, in all respects, to the theological
" system inculcated by the general institution The only practica-
" ble security for unity of theological opinion among candidates for
" orders, consists in the course of studies prescribed by the House
" of Bishops, and in the general regulations of the Convention "—
From this quotation it is evident that, in the opinion of that right
reverend gentleman, Diocesan Seminaries placed, as that of Maryland is, under the established regulations of the church, will be far
from interfering with the usages, or destroying the unity of our
zion.   Such consequences, he intimates, are much more likely to
result from the General Seminary itself In such consequences, he
asserts, a general institution in another communion in this country,
has already eventuated ; and we sincerely believe that this would be
an early consequence of an attempt to render the establishment in
New York exclusive of all others It seems to us to be too late in
the day to question the expediency of these local schools They
have the voice of the church in their favour , and, if we mistake not,
they are kindly viewed under some of their shapes by our own
Bishop. In one of his late addresses which has been published,
he congratulates the people of his charge on the provision which
has been made for theological education in the university of Maryland, by the appointment of Dr Wyatt as a Professor of Divinity in
that institution We rejoice with the Bishop in every distinction
which is conferred on this amiable and excellent brother, and we
hope and trust that his appointment may be salutary to the church,
for the welfare of which he is deeply interested But though our
Diocesan is favourable to this form of professorships, which is not
only " independent of the General Seminary," but without the juris-
diction of our Conventions, yet let us not be misunderstood ,—we
would not for a moment insinuate that the President of our Convention has any private partialities or secret regard for that plan of
education which the late Convention adopted, and which, as its

agents, we are now advocating   He has annihilated every expecta-
tion of this kind, when, though he did not say that "the intentions of
those who planned and promoted this scher were *disrespectful or
rebellious*," he nevertheless did pronounce the scheme itself to be
unconstitutional and disorganizing—Yet in his Pastoral, page 23,
line 10, we find him expressing himself thus : " That there should
" be a Seminary in Maryland, I am far from being prepared to deny.
" That as many young men as possible should be educated for the
" church, is certainly my most ardent wish and my daily prayer "—
Why then, it may be asked, all this opposition to a scheme which is
designed to accomplish the object of his wishes and his prayers'—
Because, he tells us, this scheme is unconstitutional, and his own
Diocess, the Dioceses of Virginia and New York, the Bishops of
both, and of Pennsylvania, the whole House of Bishops, the Convention of Clerical and Lay Deputies, to the contrary notwithstanding,
he is of the same opinion still

He who finds fault with a plan, should be prepared to suggest, as
a substitute, something less exceptionable In the present case,
were the measures of the late Convention to be abandoned, what
preferable course would be proposed ? The pastoral letter does
not explicitly state any . but we may, without fear of error, under-
take to name the resolution on this subject which would soon grace
our journals—a resolution to solicit the privilege of establishing in
this Diocess a branch of the Seminary in New York. And what
would be the form, and the operation, and the advantages of this
branch ? Under whose government would it be placed ? Under
our Convention—under our Bishop ? By no means; but under a
Board of Trustees—to reside, where ? In Maryland ? We might
have some " six or seven," whilst New York is to have at present
four and twenty, all of whom may be residents of that city , less than
one-half of which number constitutes a quorum for the transaction
of all business—and her influence in the Board is, to increase in
proportion to the pecuniary contributions of the wealthy and liberal
members of her communion Where are these meetings to be
held ? New York again, where the business of the Board is to be
conducted, and where few, if any, of the small number of Trustees
which we are permitted to have, can seldom, if ever, conveniently
attend What privilege, then, we again ask, is Maryland to enjoy

from the establishment of this branch? The privilege of supporting an institution, in the management of which, she can scarcely be heard—the privilege of contributing to procure the honour of having a New York School of a subordinate character established within our limits! And is there in such a school any thing so attractive and promising as to induce us, for it, to relinquish a Seminary formed in accordance with the general principles of the church, capable of being accommodated to the peculiar regulations of our own Diocess, and the management of which rests in a Board of Trustees appointed by, and under the control of, our own Convention? If the voice of a large majority, of so large and respectable a meeting as that of June last, is to be regarded as any expression of the opinion and wishes of the Episcopalians throughout the state, the language of Maryland is decidedly in favour of a Diocesan Theological Seminary

But to proceed The constitution of the General Seminary has been produced, analyzed and extolled in the pastoral letter of our Diocesan, and a contrast has been instituted, intended to militate against the constitution of the state Seminary On this comparison we forbear to remark, comparison is an invidious task We believe there are excellences in the constitution of the General Seminary; we wish it were altogether unexceptionable, and we do most sincerely join that Board in praying for the prosperity of the institution intrusted to their care, and in supplicating for all who are in any way connected with it the salutary influences of the spirit of truth and holiness. With these observations we pass the contrast by, expressing our cordial wish that between the two institutions nothing but a spirit of unity, peace, and concord may ever prevail, and that they may know no other emulation but to do good and to extend the interests of the Redeemer's kingdom.

With respect to those detached, definite objections which the Bishop has urged, these we deem it our duty to notice briefly. a brief explanation will, we think, show that they are premature and fallacious —His first stricture on our constitution relates to the power of the Board with regard to the appointment or dismissal of a Professor —It is objected, that any Professor may be voted in or out without ceremony by a majority of the number of Trustees who form a quorum The assertion with regard to the dismission of a Professor is a gratuitous inference On this subject the Convention has not yet legislated The difficulty however, if it be one, is now provided for, in the By-Laws of the Board,* which, together with the proceedings of the Board, are all subject to the revision and control of any succeeding Convention of the Diocess. This we think, is an important provision; it secures the proper management of the Seminary so long as the Convention itself remains sound in faith and morals· should that body become corrupt, then all the checks which human ingenuity could devise would prove inefficient.

This consideration fully and fairly, meets the next objection also, an objection which rests on the ungenerous suspicion that this Seminary is a "systematized" design to introduce into the church, doctrines repugnant to its articles —If such were indeed the design of its promoters, then why did they make it a leading article in their constitution that "no course of study shall be appointed, which shall be inconsistent with the course laid down by the General Convention?" Why did they give to the Convention of this state an express power of revision over all the acts of the Board Trustees? These are restraints with which disaffected and designing men, would not willingly bind themselves, they are the evidences of that liberal, honest spirit, that spirit of attachment to the doctrines, discipline and usages, of our venerable church, which influenced the Convention in devising and promoting this plan —In the note, we subjoin the names of those who voted for this plan —With the character, the principles and the standing of these men, the members of this Dio-

---

* *By Laws* —"1st No person shall be appointed a Professor in this Seminary, unless his nomination be made at one meeting of the Board, and acted upon at a subsequent meeting, due notice of the business of this meeting being given to each member of the Board, at least six weeks, before it is to be entered upon

2d When a Professor is considered as unworthy of his office, he shall be dismissed by a vote of the Board of Trustees But he shall not be removed from office, unless the proposition to that effect be made at one meeting of the Board, and acted upon at a subsequent one, due notice of the business of this meeting being given to each member of the Board, at least three months before it is to be entered on

less are generally acquainted,* these are the men who have been publicly charged with "*rushing* into the establishment of an institution at variance, with a principle fixed by the General Convention, and placing it under a constitution which was hastily conceived, ardently pressed and inconsiderately adopted."—Can such a charge be sustained? Will it be countenanced? Thus much with regard to this declaration, so far as it bears upon the acts of the Convention — Those reflections which are cast upon the clergy of a particular section of our Diocess, and upon our young brethren in the ministry, we do not deem it incumbent upon us to answer Brethren, we have done We have discharged an unpleasant task, to which we were publicly and imperiously called, we have endeavoured, in a respectful manner, to furnish you with such information as this subject demanded, and which would serve to correct any erroneous impressions which might have been made upon your minds, by partial statements which may have reached you.

* Those who voted in the affirmative.

Clergy	Laity.
Rev Chas Mann,	T. G. Addison,
Ethan Allen,	N. Ridgely,
L J Ellis,	Clement Brooke,
Wm Hawley,	John Thomas,
H L Davis, D. D	John Poole,
T G Allen,	Francis Lowndes,
N Young,	Sam Ridout,
W D. Addison,	Mordecai Booth,
J Johns,	Robert Crane,
J P K. Henshaw,	John C Herbert,
P T Smith,	Geo D Parnham,
W. Armstrong, Jr	H G S Key,
J. R Keech,	J Cottman,
J. R. Walker,	Jas Brawner,
S C Stratton,	Richard Potts,
I Allen,	Thos Gardiner,
J L Bryan,	Jonathan Duley,
C P McIlvaine,	Jas Stuart,
S H Tyng,	F S Key 19
G Aisquith,	
W Wickes,	
B P Aydelotte,	
R H Mitchell, 2?	

C

The church of Maryland, has therefore, in the exercise of a constitutional right, resolved, to call upon her members, for the means of providing education and support for pious candidates for orders in her ministry, in an institution, governed exclusively by her Convention, located within her limits, and endowed and supported by the benefactions of her members and their christian brethren.

Appointed to carry this interesting plan into effect, we earnestly appeal to your feelings as men, to your obligations and privileges as christians We ask you to enable us to lead to the altars of our God, those who are sincerely solicitous to serve him in the ministry of his Son. We ask you to aid us in preparing for their education at home, that we may retain them in our own circles, and experience the comfort, and the salutary influence of the presence and example of these children of the church, whilst they are training, as the champions of the cross. We ask to be relieved from sending them—the few who can afford to go, to other and distant sections of our widely extended country

We solicit at your hands, the means of providing for the supply of those who are hungering for the bread of life

We appeal to the members of our church, and to all interested in her prosperity, to aid us in placing the church in Maryland, upon a level in point of privileges with the station which she has attained in other Dioceses

Our petition is for no common object—it is for a portion, for the sons of God, and for a provision to extend the kingdom and multiply the faithful and efficient ministers of that Redeemer, who purchased the church with his own blood

Believing that you will be ready to distribute, willing to communicate, we pray God to accept and bless your offerings, and to sanctify them to the good of souls, and to the honour of our God and Saviour

At a meeting of the Board of Trustees, held in Georgetown, June 11th, 1822,—the following resolution was offered.

"Whereas an opinion has been declared by the Rt Rev Bishop, that the sense of the church of Maryland, was not fairly and sufficiently expressed, by the late Convention, in the establishment of a

Theological Seminary for this Diocess, and as it has also been represented to us, that some dissatisfaction exists on this subject with
some members of the church, who contemplate applying to the
Bishop, to call a special Convention for the purpose of attaining a
more full expression of the sense of the church on this interesting
subject.

"Therefore, *Resolved*, That the Board with a view of promoting,
harmony and union in the church, and giving opportunity to those
who may desire it, will suspend, until the 1st day of September next,
all further proceedings under the act of the Convention for the establishment of a Theological Seminary, and that a committee be appointed to prepare an address from the Board to the church of Maryland, in which proper and respectful notice be taken of the pastoral letter of the Bishop on this subject, and the whole matter be fairly
laid before the members of the church for their consideration "

On this resolution it may be well to remark, that the Board entertained no doubt with regard to the sense of the Diocess on the subject of a Theological Seminary, or the constitutional right of the late
Convention to establish it, they were perfectly satisfied to discharge
the duties to which that Convention appointed them, and from the
experiment which had been made, their hopes of collecting adequate
funds were sanguine —Yet, to satisfy the few who were discon-
tented,—to show them, that they are not disposed to disregard the
feelings of a single member of their communion, when those feelings
can be consulted without sacrificing duty,—they passed the resolution   The Board now wait the result   If a special Convention is
called, they are confident that it will reiterate, in louder tones, an
approbation of the course which has been already prescribed   If no
special Convention be summoned, they shall take for granted, that
those for whom the above resolution was passed, have satisfied themselves of the sentiments of this Diocess in some other way, and they
will go forward, regarding it as a tacit admission, that the voice of
Maryland is in favour of a Diocesan Theological Seminary

The address referred to in the resolution, is the address which
covers the preceding pages, having been prepared by a member of

the committee, it was read to the Board and *unanimously* adopted, the following members being present.

Revd. Dr. DAVIS,

„ Mr HENSHAW,

„ „ WELLER,

„ „ HAWLEY,

„ „ JOHNS,

„ „ M'ILVAINE,

„ „ TYNG,

FRANCIS S. KEY, Esq.

Dr THOMAS HENDERSON.

CLEMENT SMITH, Esq

CONSTITUTION

OF

The Theological Seminary of the Protestant Episcopal Church of Maryland.

ARTICLE I

OF THE MANAGEMENT OF THE SEMINARY

The management of this Seminary shall be vested in a Board of Trustees, who shall have power to constitute professorships, appoint Professors, prescribe the course of study, make by-laws for the government of the Seminary, provided, that no such by-laws shall be inconsistent with the Canons of the General Convention and the Diocesan regulations under which this Seminary is established, and that no course of study be appointed which shall be inconsistent with the course laid down by the General Convention

ARTICLE II

The Board of Trustees shall consist of eight Clergymen and five Laymen, who shall be elected triennially by a ballot of the Convention, and shall continue to act as such until their successors are appointed, and the Bishop of the Diocess shall be *ex officio* President of the Board of Trustees

ARTICLE III

The regular meetings of the Board of Trustees shall be semi-annual, at such times and at such places as they may think proper. They may also from time to time hold any occasional meetings which they may think expedient.

ARTICLE IV

The Board of Trustees shall choose out of their own number a Vice President. They shall also choose a Secretary and Treasurer, whose duty it shall be, to execute such duties as may, consistently with this constitution, be required of them

ARTICLE V

The President, or in case of his inability to act, the Vice President shall, at the request of any two Clerical and one Lay Trustees, call, by circular letter, a special meeting, four Clerical and three Lay Trustees shall form a quorum for the transaction of business

ARTICLE VI

It shall be the duty of the Secretary to submit the records of the Board to the inspection of the Convention, at every annual meeting of that body, and at any other times when the said Convention may call for them, and it shall also be the duty of the Secretary, or any member of the Board whom they may appoint, to make a report to every annual meeting of the Convention of the state of the Seminary in all its departments.

ARTICLE VII

The Board of Trustees shall have power to supply any vacancies which may occur in their body, during the recess of the Convention, provided the elections made under the authority of this article be laid before the Convention at the next meeting after such elections have taken place, to receive their approval

ARTICLE VIII.

All the acts of the Board of Trustees shall be subject to the revision of the Convention, and the votes of two-thirds of the members present at the Convention shall be sufficient to annul any one of their proceedings The Convention may propose any business for the deliberation of the Board.

ARTICLE IX.

The number of Professors in the Seminary shall be increased or diminished as the funds may justify and the number of students or other circumstances may require. No one shall be appointed as a Professor in the Seminary who is not a Presbyter in full standing in the Protestant Episcopal Church of the United States

ARTICLE X.

The location of the Seminary shall be determined by the Convention, and any resolution to change it shall be proposed at one Convention and determined at the Convention next ensuing And to effect any such alteration, the concurrence of two-thirds of the members present shall be required.

ARTICLE XI.

Alterations and amendments to this Constitution, shall only be carried by being proposed to one Convention, published in the journals of that Convention, and passed by the vote of the succeeding Convention

BY-LAWS,

FOR

The Regulation of the Theological Seminary of the Episcopal Church in Maryland, and of the Board of Trustees appointed for its government.

ARTICLE I

OF THE BOARD OF TRUSTEES.

Sec 1 The semi-annual meetings of the Board, shall be held, the first, on the day preceding the day of the annual meeting of the Convention; the second, six months after the first The first shall be held where the annual meeting of the Convention takes place; the second, where the Seminary is located These, and all other meetings of the Board, shall be opened and closed with prayer

Sec 2 The President of the Board shall have a right to suggest such business as he may think proper for the consideration of the Board,—to take part in the discussion of all questions, which may come before them, and to vote on all occasions

Sec 3 The Board of Trustees shall hold an annual examination of the students upon those branches of study which they shall have attended to in the Seminary This examination shall be held at the second semi-annual meeting of the Board

Sec. 4 The Board shall inspect the fidelity of the Professors, and especially be watchful of their private characters and the consistency of their faith and practice, with the doctrine and discipline of the Protestant Episcopal Church, in the United States of America It shall also be the duty of the Board to watch over the conduct of the Students, to redress grievances, and to examine into the whole course of instruction and study, in the Seminary.

ARTICLE II

OF THE PROFESSORS

Sec 1 No person shall be appointed a Professor in this Seminary unless his nomination be made at one meeting of the Board, and acted upon at a subsequent meeting, due notice of the business of this meeting being given to each member of the Board, at least six weeks before it is to be entered upon

Sec 2 When a Professor is considered as unworthy of his office, he shall be dismissed by a vote of the Board of Trustees But he shall not be removed from office, unless the proposition to that effect be made at a meeting of the Board, and acted upon at a subsequent one, due notice of the business of this meeting being given to each member of the Board, at least three months before it is to be entered on

Sec 3 Any Professor, intending to resign his office, shall give six months notice of such intention, to the Board of Trustees

Sec 4 The Professors shall have power to suspend or dismiss from the Seminary, any Student whom they may consider, on any account whatever, a dangerous or unprofitable member of the institution But in all cases of suspension or dismission, an appeal may be made to the Board of Trustees

Sec 5 The Professors may regulate the times and subjects of their recitations and lectures as they may think proper All meetings of the students for recitation, shall be opened with prayer by the attending Professor

Sec 6 The Professors are required, by all the means in their power, to cherish and promote among the students, an unreserved devotion to God, a thorough and practical acquaintance with experimental religion a spirit of enlightened, fervent, and expanded zeal, in the cause of Christ a strong attachment to the doctrines, discipline, and liturgy of the Episcopal Church, and in a word, all those spiritual and divine gifts, without which, their ministry cannot be useful to the cause of religion

ARTICLE III
OF THE STUDENTS

Sec 1 Every Student, applying for admission into the Seminary, shall produce satisfactory testimonials that he possesses good natural talents that he is of a prudent and discreet deportment is in full communion with some Christian Church, and has obtained those literary qualifications, which are required by the Canons of the General Convention, of those who apply to be admitted as candidates for holy orders

Sec 2 It is expected of every Student, that he will place before him the glory of God and the salvation of souls, as the great objects in all his studies and labours, that he will depend on the Holy Scriptures and the grace God, for his principal and essential qualifications for the Gospel Ministry and that under deep conviction that all mental qualifications will be comparatively of little value to the church, unless they be united with enlightened devotion, and fervent piety He will consider it a primary duty as a Student of Theology, to "grow in the grace and in the knowledge of our Lord and Saviour Jesus Christ" Every Student, at his admission into the Seminary, shall subscribe the following declaration "Under "a solemn impression of the importance of improvement in know- "ledge and piety, in order to a proper preparation for the Gospel "Ministry, I solemnly promise, in dependence upon the help of "God that I will diligently attend upon all the instructions of this "Seminary that I will conscientiously conform to all the regulations "enacted for its government, and will readily yield to all the lawful "requisitions and wholesome admonitions of its Trustees and Profes- "sors, while I shall continue a member thereof"

Sec 3 The regular period of continuance in the Seminary shall be three years. At the end of this time, a Student may receive a written certificate of approbation, and of a full Theological education, according to the course of the Seminary, from under the hands of the Professors. But this is not to prevent any from entering the Seminary, and enjoying its instructions, for a shorter time than three years

Sec 4 Every Student shall write on such subjects as may be prescribed to him by the Professors. Once in every month each Student shall commit to memory a piece of his own composition, and pronounce it before the Professors and Students, for their remarks and criticism upon the piece and the manner of its delivery

Sec 5 There shall be two vacations in the Seminary: one to commence on the day after the adjournment of the autumnal semi-annual meeting of the Board of Trustees, and continue for three weeks, the other to commence on the day after the other semi annual meeting of the Board, and to continue for six weeks

ARTICLE IV
OF THE FUNDS

Sec 1 All sums subscribed to this institution, exceeding $100, shall be invested in a permanent fund, which shall be placed at interest and suffered to accumulate till it yields an annual income, adequate to the support of at least one Professor. Donations and annual subscriptions of a less sum than $100, shall be liable to disbursement, for the support of Professors and other expenses of the Seminary, and if there be any surplus, it shall be added to the permanent fund

Sec 2 The Treasurer of this institution shall invest the funds not liable to immediate disbursement, in some safe and productive stocks, and shall hold the disposable funds subject to the order of the Board. He shall also give bonds, with good and sufficient securities, for the faithful discharge of the duties of his office

Sec 3 No moneys may be received by any person, from the funds of this Seminary, without an order upon the Treasurer, signed by the financial committee, which committee, consisting of three members, shall be appointed by the Board

Sec 4 The Treasurer shall lay before the Board, at each semi-annual meeting, an account of the state of the funds, and of the particular receipts and expenditures on account of the Seminary

Sec. 5 The intention and directions of testators, or donors, in regard to moneys, or other property, left or given to the Seminary, shall be sacredly regarded. The sum of $15,000 shall be sufficient to endow a professorship. The sum of $2,000 shall be sufficient to endow a scholarship. If any individual, or number of individuals not greater than three, shall found or endow a professorship, or a scholarship, or a fund to be applied to special purposes, said professorship, scholarship, and fund, shall severally be called by such names as the individuals who founded or endowed them may direct

Printed in the USA
CPSIA information can be obtained
at www.ICGtesting.com
LVHW080202160823
755395LV00020B/331

9 781275 860650